Peter

Forgot to give this
to you on the back o

Remember you're a
wonderful dad, man a
generally splendid you
being. Be more!

love

Bee
& Colette

How to Outshine the Rest

Sensible, Practical, and Useful Things You Need to Know to Improve Your Career and Business Dramatically

REBECCA BONNINGTON

ISBN: 978-1-4834-0952-8 (sc)
ISBN: 978-1-4834-0951-1 (e)

Library of Congress Control Number: 2014904866

Lulu Publishing Services rev. date: 03/21/2014

CONTENTS

ACKNOWLEDGEMENTS

There have been many great teachers in my life and I would like to thank them all for their positive influence, which got me where I am today: happy, fulfilled, and loving the work I do.

Let us start at the beginning with Mrs Harrison and Mrs Critchlow – both firm, but fair, primary school teachers. Then, Mrs Harris, my sixth form tutor – a real rock during a very stormy time; Garry Mason, my first line manager, a personnel manager from the old school, and a brilliant mentor; Muriel Gilbride, now sadly departed from this world, but her positive leadership style remains with me even today; Peter Taylor, CBE, of The Town House Collection who gave me his time freely to help me understand that you can be a decent human being and run a successful business; Jonathan Clark, my first NLP (Neuro-Linguistic Programming) teacher on whose course I finally found peace; Dr Richard Bandler, John La Valle, and Kathleen La Valle, who taught me how to master NLP and rather than do it, live it. The work of Dr Richard Bandler influenced many of the tools and techniques described in this book.

Also, to my big brother, who had his first book published last year, which spurred me on, in true sibling rivalry, to crack on with mine, and to my mum (1944-2012) who remained strong through the toughest of times. She brought me up to be independent in mind and spirit, taught me to always stand up for what you believe in and to face bullies head on. She was a single parent in the 1970s before it was common. She worked hard to support my brother and me and did a grand job.

Thanks to my wonderful, patient husband who remains stoical when I say I am off to Florida for a week's training and that now I am writing a book. His love, kindness, and support are appreciated greatly.

Thanks, also, to my children, Lottie, Charlie, and Ruby, who give me so much joy and pleasure. They are wonderful human beings who I know will help make a positive difference to the world no matter what path they choose.

INTRODUCTION

For many years I have worked with senior businesspeople and no matter the size of their organization, their industry, or how many people they lead or employ, there is one single common denominator: they are people. Real human beings with real needs, wants and desires, and real problems or conundrums that they need to overcome.

Often, these people have areas in their working lives where they are under confident, unsure, or unskilled and this is where I come in.

Individuals and organizations come to me because I teach teams and individuals how to think differently. I also teach them how to develop emotional intelligence and how to ask the right questions to get the responses they want. They learn how to become exquisite communicators in a very short space of time so that they can influence, work with, sell, promote, relate to and lead anyone, anywhere and at any time (a bit like the Martini advert in the 1970s).

The way I do this is to use common sense, which is surprisingly uncommon, and superb tools and techniques taken from the world of Neuro-Linguistic Programming (NLP) and my own career as a managing director. The results are impressive. The vast majority of my clients achieve what they set out to in the timescales they set themselves and the good habits stay with them. Years later, my clients are still using and benefitting from the things I helped them learn, so I know it works.

I am a practical Mancunian and, as such, I believe spades should definitely be called spades and that keeping it simple is the best way forwards for pretty much anything we do, except perhaps brain surgery which does seem to be a tad complicated. When it comes to business and your relationships with those people with whom you work, simplicity is always the best policy. I have lost count of the number of situations I have worked on with clients where they have over complicated everything and tied themselves in great big knots when all they needed to do was slice through the knot and get straight to the point.

It is for this reason you will find this book completely void of jargon, acronyms, technical speak or anything else that is designed to alienate and confuse. What you will find is simple, clear language that we all use in our normal, everyday lives. I will not ask you to cascade anything, to extend your bandwidth or to do any blue sky thinking because let us face it, all of that is utter nonsense, usually invented by people who want to add a few zeroes to their consultancy invoice.

This book is for you if you are ambitious, keen to learn, wish to be an exquisite communicator, work, own a business, lead a business, manage people, or simply wish to improve yourself and be even better at the things you do, and maybe even try a few new things.

Your mind needs to be open, so open it now and as you turn each page, read with the curiosity of a child learning something new and enjoy the difference that you discover within yourself. Surprise yourself at what you can do and achieve by simply using your brain.

Use this book as a one-off read and then as a book to refer back to when needed. View it as your coaching companion, something to refer to when you are stuck for an answer or for when you are in need of inspiration. You can read the book in any order, but on your first read follow the chapters in the correct order and that way it will make more sense to you.

Above all, practice, because the only difference between a novice and an expert is practice. When I began my journey as a business owner and now a leadership coach and trainer I knew very little about communication, leadership, NLP, or team working. Almost fifteen years later I know a great deal more because I read books, articles, listened to and watched experts, asked lots of questions, had a go at things, and made countless mistakes. There is always more to learn and more to discover about the world and yourself so enjoy your progress and have some fun because when you have fun you learn more, think better, and get much better results for yourself.

Your working life is something to be enjoyed. If you do not enjoy it for a prolonged period of time, go and do something that you do enjoy because a good life is so interconnected with work. I refer to it as "lifework" throughout this book. Work is to be lived, not endured.

CHAPTER ONE

The Basics: Start With the End in Mind

Every year, millions of us plan our annual holidays. This might be a traditional family holiday to somewhere sunny or it could be an adventure to an exotic location. Whichever it is, you will spend a great deal of time and energy thinking about it, planning it, researching it, and asking people questions about it. You will check out Trip Advisor, no doubt, and learn what other people already know about your chosen destination.

We do this as a matter of course. In the same way, when we are looking for someplace new to live, we check out the area, talk to people who have lived there or live nearby, we look around and imagine ourselves living there. This is something we all do. You probably did it before accepting your current job or setting up the business you currently run. You pictured yourself in that office or working in that location or actually physically doing the job you now do. You probably ran an imaginary film reel in your head and you may well have added color, noise and, if you are really into detail, you might have added smells and tastes, too. This picture would have created a feeling within you; perhaps you have that same feeling right now as you read and conjure up those images that helped you make your decision.

Some people might have talked to themselves about the new job; they might have conducted long conversations in their head about it. Others might have needed to talk to lots of other people about it before they made the final decision; some people need sounding boards to help confirm to them that what they are doing is good for them.

Others may simply have got a good feeling. When they went for the interview, they sensed that the building felt right or got a good vibe from the people they met. These people probably have a strong sense of what they will be doing in their new role and grasp the concepts of it quite quickly.

Most of us do this in one way or another for short term events such as a holiday or starting a new project and, yet, we do not always do it when we think about our long term futures. When I work with clients, the first thing I do after asking them, "What do you want?" is to get them to picture themselves doing the thing that they want to achieve. Some of my finance, IT, legal, and engineering clients will look at me strangely and tell me that they are not good at picturing things in their heads.

My response is always the same: "Tell me what your front door looks like." Amusingly enough, even the most analytical, supposedly black-and-white thinker can get a clear, rich, focused image of their front door and describe it to me in great detail.

Go ahead and try it. Think about the color, shape, size, materials, glass, wood, plastic, metal, where the letterbox is, where the handle is, whether there is a number on it, etc.

See, it is easy. All you need to do is put your mind to it.

As you think about your front door, you may notice that you can hear the bell, hear it close, and notice the sound it makes when someone knocks on it. At the same time, you may discover that this creates a feeling within you. Take a moment to locate the feeling in your body.

While this may be the first time you have ever purposefully and consciously pictured anything in such detail, as well as thinking about noises and feelings associated with the image, it is something your brain has always done, whether you are aware of it or not.

Now that you have a new skill, or have refined an existing skill, you will apply it to what you want.

Find a place where you can sit quietly and concentrate. Take a piece of paper or a notebook and a pen and answer the following questions about what it is you want from your life and your work. When I use these questions with my coaching clients, I call them "successful outcome questions" because they point you in the right direction: namely, success. Make sure you focus entirely on what you want. For example, stating, "I do not want work in this crummy office anymore," is hopeless. Learning to use your brain to create change in achieving your business and career objectives is the single most important thing you can do and it starts with your language. Before you answer the questions, I am going to make sure you understand why it is so important to answer them positively and focus precisely on what you want.

Your brain will focus on what you tell it to focus on. It is like when you decide to buy a new car or move house and you start looking at certain makes and models of car or specific areas to live in. When you decide on a particular car or area, you suddenly start seeing more of that type of car on the road or suddenly start being aware of news or information about that area.

It is not magic, there is no big secret, and there are no angels guiding you. It is a nifty mechanism in your brain called the reticular activation system and it focuses on what you instruct it to. This is why people are fond of saying, "You get more of what you focus on." It is true. Giving your brain the instruction that you "do not want to work in this crummy office," your brain will simply pick up on not working in the crummy office and it will not look for alternatives because you have not given it the instruction of what you *do* want.

Another way to illustrate this, for those who are still a little skeptical, is this little exercise: "I do not want you to think of a pink elephant." I am going to repeat that instruction so that you definitely have it: "I do not want you to think of a pink elephant."

Now, you definitely have an image of a pink elephant in your head and you are desperately trying to cross it out. Too late, you have already given your brain the instruction. Your brain does not get the "do not" bit, it just gets the "pink elephant" bit in the same way your brain will be stuck with "work in a crummy office" if that is what you state you do not want.

Stating what you want positively is a new skill to many people. You may observe that those people around you who are happy, fulfilled, content and successful in their world usually state what they want positively. This type of person normally speaks in ways that describe what they want, how they want it, and when they want it. They are clear in their language and always state it positively.

If you do not already do this, then you might like to start practicing this particular skill. Like all things that are worth learning, it takes practice, and you will only succeed by listening to yourself and taking care of how you speak.

To recap before you answer the following questions:

1. State what you want clearly, specifically, and positively
2. Focus more on what you want

A final tip is to be careful in what you wish. It might be nice to say, "I want to be a millionaire by the time I am thirty," but you have not specified how. This is vital because, if you do not specify how, then this is just an outlandish pipe dream. Alternatively, you might become a millionaire because your nearest and dearest died leaving you a million pounds or you received the fortune in compensation because you were in a horrific accident. I am sure neither of these scenarios is what you want.

So, for the "I want to be a millionaire by the time I am thirty" wish, you need to add things such as: by building a successful widget business or by working my way to the top of X Corporation or by inventing a gadget that helps people focus more on what they want. The observant among you will have noticed that I did not include winning the lottery. This is because winning the lottery is something that is completely out of your control and is an extremely pointless thing to want. Play the lottery if you wish, but remember it is a game of pure chance and *nothing* you do will affect the outcome, unlike your Successful Outcomes questions and answers.

Let us go back to starting with the end in mind:

1. Stated positively, what do you want? *Make sure this is something you can control.*
2. Why do you not have it already?
3. What will you see, hear, feel, smell, or taste when you have it? *Make sure you write a full description of this so that if a stranger read it, they understand exactly what you describe.*

4. What tangible evidence do you need to prove that you have what you want? *This could be a piece of paper, someone saying something, giving you something. Whatever it is, it must be a real, external, tangible thing.*

5. Is the thing you want good for you? Is it good for your family and friends? Is it good for your colleagues? Is it good for the wider world? *Make sure your answer is "yes" to all of these, otherwise go back and re-think what you want.*

6. For what purpose do you want this? *Notice this question is "For that purpose do you want this?" and not "Why do you want it?"*

7. What will you gain or lose when you have it?

8. Is what you want worth what you might lose by getting it?

Keep your answers safe and choose a time in the future when you want to look back and check your progress. Sign and date the answers. It is even better to say these things aloud, so that all your senses are used; you physically wrote them, you looked at them, and then you heard them. We do not need to smell or taste the paper you have written them on, but you can associate these outcomes with nice smells and tastes, perhaps a cup of coffee while you are writing, for example.

You can use these questions for any aspect of your lifework. They are useful in project planning, creating a career plan, or anything else that you would like to achieve in lifework. Keep a copy with you, as you never know when you will need them.

You might wonder whether this actually works. Yes, it does. I write my Successful Outcomes answers about once every two years and I look back to see whether I have achieved what I want. Generally, I achieve about eighty percent of what I want and often have achieved other exciting things along the way, too. I have grown my coaching and training practice by using these questions and have helped all my clients do the same. At the end of each coaching relationship we check to see whether the outcomes have been achieved or are on their way to being achieved and the answer is almost always "yes."

It is interesting to note that I enjoy the journey of achieving my outcomes. The outcomes are not the end for me, but merely a continuation of a fulfilled and happy work life. When you enjoy the journey, the outcome appears as if by magic and, often, I have not even noticed it because I have had so much fun getting there. I set these Successful Outcomes questions when I started my master's degree at the beginning of 2011; my visualization was of me at the graduation ceremony. I had relished the journey (not an easy one), so I did not care about going to the ceremony because it was no longer important to me. However, I did go because I had instructed my brain eighteen months before that this was the evidence I needed to confirm that I had an M.Sc. in Coaching. I punched the air while on stage after picking up my piece of paper and it felt fantastic, but it was merely a continuation of my lifelong journey of fulfilment and success in lifework.

Just writing down your answers is only the start of the process. The next step enables you to embed those desired outcomes firmly in your brain. This next stage of programming your brain involves a timeline (Bandler, NLP Seminars International Ltd, training manuals, 2008, 2012). Some of you may be familiar with the concept of a timeline. However, for those who are not, this is how it works:

Think about something you did yesterday, something that you do every day and is a mundane activity. It could be cleaning your teeth, eating breakfast, or drinking your first cup of tea or coffee of the day. In thinking of it, your brain had to make a picture of the activity. Now, locate that picture. Is it in front of you, behind you, to the left or right, up or down? Think of the activity again and notice where it appears. It might be helpful to think of your head as the centre of a compass, with all the coordinates coming from your head outwards.

When you have located the picture of this mundane activity, you can move onto the next stage.

Now, think about something further back in your past, such as last Easter, last Christmas, your last birthday, or your last holiday. Make sure the event has happy memories attached to it and that it happened at least four or five months ago. Notice where this picture appears.

Now think of a happy event far back in your past, perhaps three, four, or even five years ago. Notice where it appears, what distance it is from you and in which direction it is.

Wherever these pictures appear represents your past timeline.

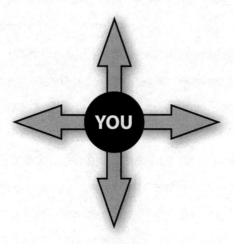

Run the same exercise for your future timeline. Think of a mundane event such as cleaning your teeth that you know for sure you will be doing tomorrow and you will know where and when you are doing it. Then select an event that you know is coming up. It could be a birthday, Christmas, a wedding, a party, or something significant that you are looking forward to with pleasure.

Similarly, select something you are looking forward to that is far off into your future. Some people plan their birthday party a year in advance or a special holiday or a wedding several years in advance. I did this exercise when I started my training and coaching business and set goals for the first year. By the end of the first year I had achieved them all, so I set some more. There is one big, audacious goal that remains a theme and all the smaller goals along the way fit in with the big one. I am still working towards the big one and having this book published is part of that.

You will have noticed by now that these future events appear in a slightly different place than your past events. It might even be in the opposite direction. If your past and future timeline are jumbled in front of you, you might find it useful to move your past timeline behind you. After all, as Richard Bandler would say, "The best thing about your past is that it is over" (Bandler, NLP Seminars International training courses, 2012).

I have found that this is often the case when people are worriers or get terribly anxious. Their future timeline jumbles with their past and all the things that did not go right for them in the past are right in front of them. When this type of thing pops up, I run a little exercise to help such people move their past timeline behind them and untangle it from their future. This way, their future is a great deal clearer and they forget many of their worries because they are behind them, mentally.

This is easy to do and simply requires a bit of space and quiet at time when you know you will not be disturbed. Start by visualizing your past timeline as you did at the very start of this exercise. Now, imagine your hands are a great big set of grappling hooks or a giant clamp and grab hold of your past timeline with both hands. Make a "clunk" noise to indicate you have attached your hands to the past timeline that you are about to move. Now, carefully and thoughtfully, move your past timeline right round to the back of your head and again fix it into place with a loud "kerrching." Release your hands from your past timeline, which is now fixed firmly in place behind you, in your past, and let go with a purposeful "click."

You might find that the vision of your future is a little clearer and that you are much less bothered by your past. Make sure this feels comfortable to you. You will know this immediately as it will feel right. If, for any reason, it does not feel right, simply move your timeline back to where it was or at least to a place that enables you to happily separate your past from your future that feels, looks, and sounds comfortable to you.

Remember those questions about successful outcomes? Look at your answers to question 3. This is where you wrote down a very clear, rich, focused image of what you will see, hear, and feel when you have achieved what you want. Think about when you want this and with whom you want it.

Now, look at your future timeline and work out where along that timeline your event or achievement is going to happen or when you would like it to happen. I recently ran this for my NLP Trainers Training. Right at the start of the course, I envisioned myself delivering a highly successful NLP Practitioner Course with eight people all loving the learning and enjoying themselves. I ran the image in my head, starting with the successful outcomes questions, and projected my desired outcome as the successful course. I found the course challenging, as well as enjoyable, and sometimes the image I made was the only thing that kept me going!

Your projected achievement might be at a less specific time than that. Use your imagination to work out when it might be or, more usefully, when you would like it to be. Make sure that this is something you can control. Putting things in your timeline that you cannot control is a fruitless exercise that will only lead to disappointment. Remember when you are thinking about what you want in life to concentrate on *you*, as you have no control over anyone except yourself.

Take the clear, rich, focused image of what you want and place it into your future. As you put it into your future make sure you click it firmly into place with a loud "click". In a seated position, keep your feet firmly on the ground and close your eyes, but only after you have read the following instructions.

1. In your mind, float up gently from your seat and look down at yourself from above. This takes a bit of practice and you will get there. Make sure you choose a comfortable, safe, and secure way to float up. Practice it now. Put the book down, keep both feet firmly on the floor, close your eyes, and float up gently out of your seat above where you are sitting. Once you have the hang of that, float up even higher to the edge of space.

2. Float along your future timeline to the place where you expect and want your achievement to happen and very carefully look

down on the event and watch yourself in the event. As you do so, notice what you say, do, and feel and what you need to learn in order to achieve your goal.

3. Now, float down very gently inside the anticipated event and have a good look through your own eyes. Again, notice anything you need to learn and take back with you to the present.

4. Once you have finished, float back up and back along your timeline, going backwards so that you notice all the necessary events that led to your achievement. This will help you realize what you need to learn, do, who you need to speak to, and what resources you will need. Remember that all your resources are in your past so you will be taking them with you back to the present.

5. Once you are satisfied that you have noted every key stage in your progress, float back down into your chair and open your eyes very gently.

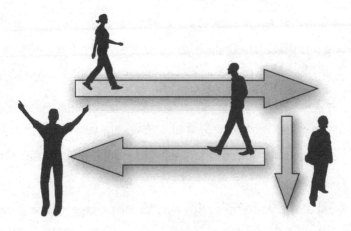

Stand up. Move around, grab yourself a drink of water, make a few calls, do a few jobs, have lots of fun, and generally distract yourself until you are ready for the next chapter.

People often ask me whether they need to keep reminding themselves of the answers to their questions and I always say, "It depends." If you are the sort of person who likes to check those answers, then please do, or you might be the sort of person, like me, who is much more in touch with their gut instinct and so does not feel the need to analyze or revisit their answers.

Figure legends

1.1 How to find your timeline.

1.2 Traveling along your timeline.

CHAPTER TWO

What is Important to You?

For nearly fifteen years, I interviewed hundreds of people in my role as a recruitment consultant and, latterly, as a managing director. I interviewed lawyers, accountants, fundraisers, sales people, property professionals, administrators, personal assistants, and many, many more types of people from different areas of business. Most of the time, the people I interviewed were happy with their chosen careers. They came to see me because they were unhappy with their boss or organization (that is for another book). However, sometimes I interviewed people who explained that they trained many years to be in their role at the level they were, but realized recently that it was not what they wanted to be doing. This is when I suggested that they climbed the career ladder, but the ladder was against the wrong wall! Usually, they laughed and that helped break any tension in the room.

Finding yourself in the wrong career is uncomfortable. If you are good, you are usually paid well, have high status in the organization and have a mortgage, kids, and a lifestyle to support, all of which might be threatened by a sudden departure from your job, a period of re-training, and starting a new career.

This chapter is also useful for those who could not think of what they wanted after reading Chapter One. I sometimes spend the first one or two sessions with a coaching client just helping them uncover what it is they actually want for themselves. Some people have never been asked what they want and some people have never realized that they can get what they want, as long as it is good for them and the people around them.

It is at this point that I draw a tree. This is my favorite model in coaching, not because I get to demonstrate my lack of artistic prowess, but drawing pictures of trees is quite therapeutic! This idea was demonstrated to me in 2005 by Heather Wright at Advance Performance.

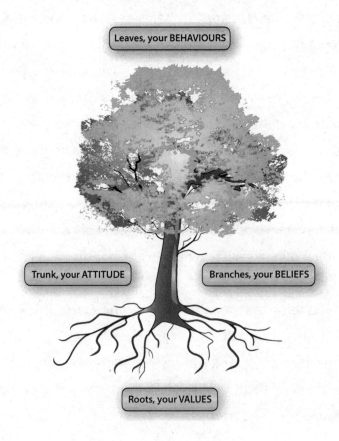

Leaves, your BEHAVIOURS

Trunk, your ATTITUDE

Branches, your BELIEFS

Roots, your VALUES

Let us start with your *values*. These are at your core and are a deciding factor in your chosen career path. The values you have are a complex combination of nature and nurture and are influenced, either negatively or positively, by the way you were brought up and the people who influenced you at a young age. Many values stem from moral codes contained within religious or spiritual belief systems. Think of the ethics you live by, whether you have a vocation, or how much importance you place on family, friends, helping others, or making money. Not all values are altruistic or particularly good for individuals or those around them. I hope that people reading this book have values that are considered ethical and that help to benefit them, those around them, and the wider community, even if it is only in a tiny way.

Your values are non-negotiable. They link so closely with your own identity that to go against your values may well cause headaches, massive stress, sickness, or eventual breakdown. This sounds a bit melodramatic, but I speak from direct and personal experience of working in an organization that considered bullying and ritual humiliation to be an acceptable form of management and it made me ill. I also worked with people who are off with stress or close to a breakdown because their employer asked them to go against their core values. They may not be consciously aware of this, but once they work through this exercise it becomes obvious.

I advise organizations to recruit people who share their values for this reason. You can have the most skilled, talented operator on the planet in your business and, for a while, they will do a brilliant job, but eventually the working relationship will break down if the organization's values and the individual's values do not match.

My values are:

1. My family
2. My business
3. My social life

Someone else's values might be:

1. Career
2. The arts
3. Friends

Another's values might be:

1. Pets/animals
2. Social life, etc.

It is essential that you put your values in order of priority because it makes decision making so much easier. My own experience of this was when Amazon called me to offer me an interview for a Leadership Consultant job. It was my dream job with an exciting company. I turned it down, though, because it was in Luxembourg and would have meant being away from home four nights a week. Since my family is my first priority, it was an easy decision to turn it down. Instead, I put all my energies into building my own leadership and corporate training business, which means I might be away five nights a month, but that is an acceptable level for my family and me.

Before you do anything else, it is essential that you work out what your values are and the order of priority in which you want to put them. The first one is the non-negotiable, come-what-may value. This process will help you decide whether your ladder is against the right wall. For example, if your core or highest value is being in the outdoors but you sit indoors all day, then it is likely that you are miserable. Similarly, if your first value is caring for others and you are an IT programmer, then you may be miserable. Sometimes, people are able to be true to their core values outside of the workplace and have enough of a balance to be happy with this. However, their workplace may not be getting the best from that person if it conflicts directly with their core values.

Do not rush this process. Take your time and live with the values you decide upon and test them out with scenarios that might pop up or came up in the past. Write them down somewhere so that when a crossroads emerges in your life, you will know exactly which direction will best suit your values.

Here is another example of my core business values in action. Here are my business values in order of priority:

1. Integrity
2. Always learning and passing that knowledge on

3. Inspiring others to learn

4. Having fun

This helps me choose the types of organizations and people I am happy to work with. In the past, my values were tested and I walked away from very well paid work because the values of certain individuals conflicted directly with mine. It was absolutely the right decision to make for me and the clients.

Attitude

Attitude is the trunk of your tree. Your attitude will be part of your overall personality; this will have emerged throughout your childhood and, in particular, during your teenage years and early twenties when you were deciding what sort of person you wanted to be. Some attitudes do not change much; a conscientious hard-worker very rarely switches to a lazy, lay-about. Others do; a rebellious rule-breaker who thinks only of themselves may well grow out of this and emerge as a kind, giving individual who works for the good of other people. Such a dramatic shift in attitude often results from a life-changing event such as maturity, illness, death, or a major catastrophe.

Disaster and life-changing events to one side, your attitude grows and develops with you as a human being, but does not often shift much. Your work ethic and attitude towards relationships and life in general tends to remain constant throughout adulthood.

I will put a caveat to this because I experienced a fundamental shift in attitude towards myself when I was 36 and learning NLP for the first time. This shift was that I finally valued myself. My work ethic remained the same and my optimistic, positive attitude towards life remained constant, but I guess my tree trunk grew a bit more and changed shape.

I advise clients when they recruit or promote to do so by gauging values and then attitude because it is another constant thing in an adult's character. Skills can be taught, so can terminology, but it takes a lifetime of experience to establish solid values and a strong attitude. Einstein said, "The only source of knowledge is experience," and he was right (Einstein, 2014).

Beliefs

Beliefs are your branches and it surprises some people that these come and go readily. Just like branches blowing off in the wind, the beliefs you held about a pop star when you were fifteen are not the beliefs you hold now as an adult. New beliefs form like new branches and old, well-established beliefs can come crashing down suddenly.

Later in this book, I will take you through the process of changing the beliefs you have that may be holding you back. For this reason, I will not go into detail about beliefs just yet.

Suffice to say, some beliefs are really useful or, in NLP terms, resourceful, while other beliefs are distinctly non-resourceful and serve very little purpose other than to hold you back from what you want to achieve.

The beliefs with which you instruct your brain enable you to spot information around you to support that belief. For example, if your favorite football team is Manchester United, then your ears prick up whenever they are mentioned and you select information about them to support your belief about how fabulous they are.

Be prepared to have your beliefs changed because what you believe to be true about the world around you will directly affect your outcomes. If, for example, you believe that everyone is a liar and a cheat, your brain will identify all the things you read, hear and experience to support that belief and you will find it difficult to experience people any other way. If you believe that the world is full of opportunity, wonderful resources, and people, then that is exactly what you will experience.

My mother was a prime example of this. When she turned fifty, she believed she was old. She kept saying things like, "Well, at my age, you can't expect...," "My age is a barrier..." and "I can't do that, I am too old." At fifty, she decided she was old and on the road to ill health. From that time, she developed a benign growth on her leg, contracted Methicillin-resistant Staphylococcus aureus (MRSA), her ankle collapsed, her arthritis worsened, her thyroid function became unstable, and eventually she got lung cancer and died of secondary liver cancer. Her world grew gradually smaller and smaller because she kept telling herself she was too old for this, that, and the other. She also kept saying things like, "I shouldn't have to do this at my age."

Now, I am not saying she might not have got all of those ailments either way, but I cannot help but the think the belief she had about herself being "too old" did not help. As Zig Ziglar said, "Positive thinking will let you do everything better than negative thinking will," (Ziglar, 2014).

If you currently hold beliefs that are wholly negative and likely to hold you back in some way, read on and be prepared to change them – now.

Behaviors

Your behaviors are your leaves. These are the most transient part of you and change according to where you are, whom you are with, and what you are doing. This is why it amazes me that organizations still insist on recruiting and promoting people based purely on observable behavior. When you are interviewing someone or in a meeting with someone, all you see is their interview or meeting "behavior." You do not see what they are like at home in front of the TV or out with their friends (perhaps this is just as well). This is why people are surprised at unusual characteristics in people who seem to behave in a "normal" way (there is no such thing as normal). When you discover that mild-mannered Steve in accounts is also, at the weekends, Stephanie at a transvestite karaoke bar, it comes as a bit of a shock. However, when you understand that the behavior you observe in the office is only Steve's "office" behavior and realize that behavior is *not* the person, you begin to realize that behaviors are only an external response to environment. No one would behave the same way on a Club 18-30 holiday as they would in the doctor's consulting room. Or, at least, I hope not.

On occasion, you might find yourself behaving oddly or out of character. If this happens, think about what is going on in your environment that is leading to this change. If necessary, take yourself out of that environment completely or change the way you respond to it.

There are people out there who display quite destructive behaviors, even in the workplace or, perhaps, especially in the workplace. While their behavior may be annoying or even threatening in some way (workplace bullies spring to mind), remember it is only their behavior that you are witnessing. Remove yourself from where the person is behaving in this way or change the way you react to them.

When I worked for a large organization, I had a boss who was very fond of bullying me. Eventually, I left that organization and started my own company. A few years later, as I walked to my office one day, we found ourselves at the same street crossing. I had not been bothered by him for a long time, so I cheerily said, "Good morning, Frank!" (Not his real name; Frank is actually my dog.) You should have seen his face! He just about managed to get a "good morning" out from his grimaced face and dashed across the road as quickly as he could. I completely changed my attitude towards him and, as a result, he was the one who was nervous of me.

Another example is of a woman who once set lawyers upon me for no good reason when I was nine months pregnant and going through a very difficult time in my business. I saw her two years later walking towards me on the same side of the road and watched as she sprinted across the road, narrowly avoiding oncoming cars in order not to have to face me. I was never scared of her or her lawyers and told her at the time to back off and, amusingly enough, she ran away then, too.

As soon as you change your reaction to unwanted or unhelpful behavior around you, that behavior dissipates. My clients feed their experience of this back to me and make observations such as, "He just does not bother me anymore," or "Their attitude completely changed towards me." As a final example, when my teenage daughter starts a stroppy, sulky tantrum, I simply laugh and her resolve crumbles as a tiny crack of a smile usually appears on her face. Then she storms off, slamming the door behind her!

This is all very well and good, but how do you actually change your attitude towards someone who is behaving in a way that is upsetting or simply driving you crazy?

This is how:

Picture the person that has been annoying or upsetting you. Hear their voice and their words and really focus on how they look when they are getting to you. Now change their voice to something ridiculous, like Donald Duck, Sylvester the Cat, or a ludicrous accent – any voice that makes you smile when you hear it.

Then imagine them really small, so small that they can fit into the palm of your hand. Shrink them right down and exaggerate some of their features like their nose, ears, and skinny or fat legs. Make them look as ridiculous as they sound. You can even dress them in silly clothes to increase their stupid appearance. Make sure you use things that make you laugh.

Now look at them in the palm of your hand and make them say something that used to annoy you in their silly voice. Tee-hee!

Keep doing it until whenever you think about them doing the things that used to bug you, you laugh. Now, whenever you see or hear them, remember the image you made of them and the voice you gave them, they will never bother you again. You might even find yourself liking them because their behavior with you will change. When it comes to working well with people, this kind of skill is really important.

I hope that this section helps you to establish where you are and whether your ladder is against the right wall. I strongly advise you to think about this part of your self-coaching carefully and make sure you are comfortable with the things you have written down. Perhaps live with those ideas for a few days or a week and come back to your notes. Once you read your notes again and if they still feel right, then go ahead and complete the rest of the exercises in the book. If things need to be altered slightly, then do that, write them down again and live with those new ones for a few days until you are completely happy that you have your ladder firmly against the right wall for you.

Figure legends

2.1 Understanding your values and more.

CHAPTER THREE

Relax to Excel

High levels of stress lead to high levels of the hormone cortisol in our bodies. What you might not know about cortisol is that it is a neuroinhibitor. I promised that there would be no jargon in this book and I am someone who sticks to their promises, however, the world of neuroscience is not full of reader-friendly terms, so I will translate: the hormone cortisol stops you from thinking straight.

You probably know this already because, when stressed, you will find it harder to remember things, to solve problems, and to work out priorities and tasks that need to be completed. You will also know that when you have been working on a problem that you cannot solve, the very best thing to do is to leave it for a while and go and do something completely different. This could be going for a walk, visiting your friends, having a shower, or simply going to bed and having a good night's sleep. My preferred method of solving problems is walking my dog. He does not care if I am slightly distant and he never asks tricky questions in the middle of my daydreaming, unlike my three demanding children! At the top of Blackford Hill I can stare out across the beautiful city of Edinburgh and, as I do so, answers usually emerge easily. I usually make a note of the idea on my iPhone so that I can remember it later.

"That is lovely," you cry, "but how on Earth do I find time to walk the dog, have a shower, or a nap in the middle of a really busy and stressful day when problems need to be solved immediately?"

The good news is that you can re-create the relaxed state of a sleep, shower, or walk in an instant, no matter where you are or what you are doing, without actually falling asleep or undressing. The other good news is that it is free, legal, and does not involve prescription drugs or alcohol. In fact, it is one of the most natural states of mind to be in and, once you get the hang of it, you will spend around 80% of your time in it. That is 80% of clear, rich, focused thinking and problem solving time while being relaxed and enjoying yourself. They should teach it in school, it is so useful.

It is called peripheral vision and those of you who study a martial art will already be aware of it and how useful it is. I am introducing it to the world of business client by client and now to a wider audience via this book. Dr Garner Thomson describes it, too, in his book *Magic in Practice*, which all medical professionals should read (Thomson, 2008). I learned it on my first NLP Practitioner course in 2006 from Jonathan Clark.

Simply sit or stand somewhere comfortable and safe. Choose a point ahead of you on a wall or in the distance and focus on it. As you do this exercise, make sure you keep your head and your eyes still. As you focus on the point ahead of you, broaden your field of vision to the left and the right of you; it is easy to do this if you imagine your favorite food or person standing just to the left and right of you.

Now do the same again, except this time widen your vision to above and below you and, at the same time, to the left and right of you. Your vision might be a little bit blurry for a moment, but your brain will soon adjust to this wider field of vision.

You now have a 360-degree view in front of you, to the side of you and above and below you so you can see more of your world. What is amazing is that you can now hear more, too, and you will be more in tune with your feelings. If there are people speaking around you, you will pick up more of their conversation.

Next, stand up and walk around the room while remaining in peripheral vision. Practice moving your focus of attention while maintaining peripheral vision and keep practicing as you go about your daily business.

What is interesting is that you will feel more relaxed, more in control, and be able to experience more of the world around you. As your body starts to relax, it will produce neuro-enhancing chemicals that, in plain English, means that you will be able to think straight. A relaxed person solves problems more effectively and efficiently and they do it with a great big smile on their face.

People often wonder why I am so happy and I can honestly say that it is because I am relaxed most of the time and this is because I live and work while in peripheral vision. It is magic.

You will find that the incessant noise and chatter you once had running through your head disappears or significantly subsides when you are in peripheral vision, which is why it is so important to practice it. Your head is clearer. Your thinking will be clearer, too, and you will actually listen and hear what is going on around you, perhaps for the first time in many years. This is what new age people call "being present." Being a practical Mancunian, I prefer to call it "really paying attention to what is going on around you" and I find it helps enormously in business because you need to be on your toes at all times.

This wonderful technique has the benefit (which we all like in business) of helping to shut your conscious mind down. For all you scientists, engineers, accountants, academics, IT professionals, and lawyers out there, shutting your conscious mind down for a change can lead to significant breakthroughs in your progress and thinking. This is because it is actually your subconscious mind that can handle millions more bits of information than your conscious mind. This is an established fact of your neurology, which is why people generally cannot hold more than seven bits of information in their head at one time. Test this by placing fifteen random items on a table, memorize them, cover them, and then try to recall as many as you can.

See, seven, tops!

The magicians who memorize an entire pack of random cards do so by attributing silly pictures or noises to each card. This means they are using their imagination, their creative brain, and delving into feelings. Feelings are contained within the limbic system of the brain. This part has no language, just feelings, and it is much easier to access a feeling than a list of numbers or types of playing cards. This is why memory is so interesting; its base is feelings rather than facts. Police officers know that no two witness statements are the same because each person will have filtered their memories through their own feelings.

When you are in peripheral vision, you are tuning out your logical, rational brain with all the language and you are tuning into the feeling, sensing brain. In this way, you are listening intensely to the person talking, you are taking everything in, and are able to respond with clarity because you are responding from your gut feeling, which is almost always right. For those who doubt me on this, just remember the last time you went against your gut feeling. It was probably a disaster and you more than likely had a sneaky suspicion that it was not right from the beginning.

The only difference between a novice and an expert in anything is practice, so practice being in peripheral vision and see what difference it makes to your life.

There are other ways of relaxing, too, and these are particularly useful just before a presentation, a bit pitch, or an interview. There are also ways of making yourself feel more powerful and in control, which is always useful when meeting with your boss, a major client, or when you are negotiating your next pay raise and promotion.

Your body is so important to how you feel and how you feel is vital to the outcomes you experience in life and work. You know this already. What you perhaps do not know is how to create feelings of power and control on purpose by altering your body posture. Altering the way you sit and stand creates chemical changes in your body. Amy Cuddy's TEDTalk, "Your body language shapes who you are," added well-researched scientific proof to this long-held assertion from the world of NLP (Cuddy, 2012).

The very first thing to do is to stand and sit up straight at all times. This helps your breathing and keeps you in a state of readiness and alertness at all times. It also helps people take you seriously. The next thing to do is make sure you sit and stand in a way that makes you appear bigger than you are. This does not mean sitting spread eagled with arms and legs all over the place, but it does mean sitting with your arms out in front on the desk or table or standing with your hands on your hips or moving your arms when you talk in a controlled and expansive manner. Think of Bill Clinton and Barack Obama with their broad hand gestures, their straight bodies, and their direct eye contact. Also, look at Margaret Thatcher and how her stance looked powerful and big. Oprah Winfrey is another great example of someone sitting and standing in powerful positions.

It is great that even if you do not feel powerful at first, you will once you adopt these broader stances because your body chemistry alters to match your power posture. Amy Cuddy discovered that testosterone increases, which is the power hormone in men and women, and cortisol decreased. Cortisol is a stress hormone that, as we know, prevents you from thinking straight. Adjusting your body so you feel more powerful helps you produce the right chemicals for improved thinking and a more confident frame of mind. Magic.

Just before a big meeting or presentation, very gently rise up onto your tiptoes and come down again. This clears your mind completely and automatically helps you feel relaxed. More magic.

Finally, presenting while you are in peripheral vision really helps and so does holding your tongue just below the roof of your mouth, a little behind your top front teeth. Imagine you have a piece of chocolate stuck to the roof of your mouth just behind your front teeth and very gently pretend to touch it with your tongue, so your tongue is just below the roof of your mouth, not quite touching. This also has the effect of switching the chatter off and helping you relax. Again, really useful for meetings and interviews when it is other the persons turn to talk. It is also useful when you need to learn something because you will be learning it unconsciously and that means it is more likely to stick.

Learning unconsciously is simply another way of saying learning effortlessly. While you are in peripheral vision, your own thoughts switch off, or, at least, quieten, which means you are listening while being present. This, in turn, means that you hear more, see more, and experience more of what is going on, which has the result that more information goes into your head and is retained.

Finally, remember to walk with purpose. A friend reminded me of this recently, as she told me she was having problems with a very senior director in her workplace not taking her seriously. I noticed that she walked with a shuffle like a small child coming up to her dad asking for candy or a new toy.

I explained to her that if she walked like a child then the big boss was more likely to treat her like a child. I got her to practice striding with purpose into the office and her whole demeanor changed instantly. So, head up, shoulders back, and focus on walking with purpose.

Even if you do not use anything else from this book, use these really simple techniques every single day at every opportunity and you will find your life is much more relaxed and easier. Your thinking will improve and so will your ability to solve problems.

I spend around 80% of my time in peripheral vision and it helps enormously with my busy life, which consists of three children, a husband, a dog, a business and, up until recently, a master's degree to complete, and a book to write! Whatever you read in this book, rest assured that I have used it, tried it, tested it, and evaluated it for myself, as well as with my clients.

The final trick I use to fool my brain into a relaxed state is to imagine myself lying on a Caribbean beach. The sky is blue, the sand is pure white, the palm trees are very gently blowing backwards and forwards in a light breeze. While I lie down with my eyes closed on a very comfortable sun lounger with plump cushions, I can hear the waves coming in and going out in a beautiful rhythm which helps me match my breathing to that rhythm. I use this when I am at the dentist. It has become so powerful and I have practiced it so much that my brain brings this image to the fore the minute I hear a dental instrument and when I lie down in the dentist's chair. I also used it recently when I had to have a CT scan and went inside a big machine that looked like something out of *Doctor Who* and felt slightly claustrophobic.

People wonder why I am relaxed in what are normally stressful situations. It is easy: I have trained my brain to think of really lovely, relaxing stuff instead. I have practiced and focused on this; although my logical brain wants to take me back to discomfort, stress, and sometimes fear, I work hard to create the image and the feelings that make me feel good. I figure it is worth it to feel good. Someone posted one of those sayings on Facebook that the world is fond of reading and it said, "It takes just as much thought to be unhappy as it does to be happy." This is so true, so what is preventing you from putting all your energy into happy ways of thinking and being?

CHAPTER FOUR

The Language of Success

Positivity

Much is written about the power of positive thinking and some of it is true. I like to stick to one simple example of why selecting your words positively makes a huge difference. It is probably something you have heard before, but as with all simple things, it is always worth repeating and reminding ourselves why we do something.

When I work with groups or individuals, I always listen out for the words they use and the emphasis they place on certain key words or phrases. One of things I notice about successful people is that they always speak positively. I do not mean that they are hopeless optimists or that they are unrealistic; what I mean is that they state what they want in positive terms.

I described this exercise in Chapter One and it is so important to get right that I am repeating it now: I want you not to think about a pink elephant. Do *not* think about a pink elephant. Whatever you do, do not think about a pink elephant.

What you will now have in your head is a vivid picture of a pink elephant and your brain is attempting to erase it. The more I write things such as, "Stop thinking of a pink elephant," the harder it is to get rid of that image of a pink elephant.

This is because our human brains find it extremely difficult to process a negative thought. Therefore, when we say, "Do not spill your milk," or "Do not send that email," our human brains hear "Spill your milk," and "Send that email." If you have children of your own then you will know exactly what I mean.

I used to work with people who wanted to lose weight and they were forever telling me that they "did not want to be fat" and that they "did not want to eat so much." I helped many of them change their language to "I want to be healthier and slimmer," and "I will eat less and exercise more." Among other things with which I helped them, this simple change of language enabled them to start thinking about what they were telling themselves.

Therefore, I wonder what you are telling yourself about your career or your business. If it is "We cannot lose this contract," or "I am not going to fail," then you might want to think about changing some of those negative words because all your brain is hearing is "Lose this contract" and "Going to fail." The successful people I work with say, "We will win the contract," and "We will succeed."

I hope that you can hear the difference saying these things makes to your feelings and, therefore, your ultimate outcomes. If I were writing a book about affirmations, then I would give you a whole list of positive things to say; however, I am not and there is much more to getting the results you want than simply saying, "I will" or "I want" and then stating clearly exactly what it is that you want.

We need to go deeper into your language patterns and to do that I need to explain two crucial models in NLP that, once learned, will change the way you use language forever or, at least, make you think twice about how you speak and write in business.

Before I do that, I want you to notice something about yourself. Everyone is different, so there is no right or wrong answer to these questions; it is simply a question of noticing what works for you and doing more of it.

Think about hobbies or pastimes that you love doing. Think about foods or activities that you absolutely love and to which you look forward. These can be things that you do with other people (you are allowed to choose consensual sex, if you like) or on your own (the sex thing might still apply!).

When you think about the stuff you love and take pleasure in, what words do you use when you are looking forward to doing it? Is it words such as *love, like, wish, desire, want, need, will, shall, must, can, do*, or some such other word?

Now think about tasks or activities that you dislike, put off, and generally avoid because you do not like doing them. For me, this is ironing. I will do anything to avoid doing the ironing and when I think about doing the ironing, I say, "I have to." This is when I know that it is something that I will put off doing for as long as possible, will rush to get through it and not do a very good job. However, I love training and coaching others and say things like, "I am going to," "I would love to," and "I will," whenever I am talking to clients or complete strangers about my work.

When you have found the thing you hate doing, think about the words you use when you are about to do it. These could be *should, must, have, cannot, will not, do not, try, would, need*. The observant among you will notice that some words feature on both lists and this is because we are all different. Some people find *must* or *need* exciting and motivating, while others find them really dull and demotivating, so it is important you find your own words that drive and excite you.

Test out your driver words and use them when thinking about things you have been putting off and listen to how differently you feel about those tasks now. You might see your to-do list in a different light.

Your voice

Most people have an inner and an outer voice. The outer voice is the one that we all hear and that you use to communicate with other people. The inner voice is weak or even non-existent in some people and really strong and powerful in others. Sometimes people will hear voices that belong to other people; quite often, these belong to parents, spouses, or teachers and are often critical. All of this is normal, so long as the voices are sane and rational. If you hear voices that are telling you to do bad things to yourself or others, then go and seek professional help immediately. Otherwise, you can turn the internal and external voices you experience to good use.

Many people waste time criticizing themselves and telling themselves that they are rubbish. This is not particularly useful or encouraging, so about six years ago I stopped doing it. Instead, I have an inner voice that tells me I am making progress every day, always learning new, useful things, and on the occasion that I do make a mistake, my inner voice asks me what I want to learn from it.

When I work with my clients, this is what I do to help them switch off any internal or external chatter that is not helping them:

Locate the voice that is proving to be negative. Is it inside or outside your head? Whereabouts is it exactly? What is the volume? What are the pitch, tone, and quality of the voice like? To whom does the voice belong? Does it fade in or fade out? Does it have a rhythm or melody to it? Write these answers down.

Once you have identified the qualities of this unhelpful noise, then you can start to change it into something more useful. Think about a really positive and encouraging voice in which you have talked to yourself or in which others have spoken to you. This might relate back to something you did brilliantly and often talk to yourself about, or for which someone gave you massive praise and encouragement, and is a voice you remember clearly as very helpful.

Answer the same questions relating to this voice about whether it is internal or external, its quality, its volume, its pitch, its pace, its melody, etc. Write these answers down.

What do you notice? Where are the differences between the unhelpful and helpful voices?

Now, start to change the unhelpful voice into a helpful one. If the unhelpful one was external, move it to an internal voice and see what happens. Does this change the way you think and feel about your career and business ahead of you? You will need to change each difference from the unhelpful to helpful voice stage by stage and check at each stage whether it is now helpful. If it is more helpful once changed, then leave it there.

I realize that some people find this easy to do and others find it harder. Whenever I work with clients who find this sort of thing a bit tricky, I go slowly and take it one baby step at a time. After all, you are doing things you have never done before and never heard of before. It is a bit like learning to read. You need to learn the letters one by one and then slowly put them together, sounding them out to make words, and you will find that once you have some simple words in your command, you can move onto ones that are more complex. Be patient with yourself, experiment, try what works, and ditch what does not. Give it a go and have some fun with it.

Building rapport with your words and voice

Clients always try to place my accent. I am from Manchester, lived in Yorkshire for five years and now in Edinburgh for 19 years, so my accent is difficult to pinpoint. However, when I speak to clients I am not always using the same voice that I would use at home or with my friends. When you were at school, you probably spoke very differently to the way you spoke at home, with more slang, more swearing, louder, quicker, and often in more dramatic tones.

You see, we naturally alter our voices depending with whom we speak. You will have heard the expression "telephone voice" and, no doubt, you have your own telephone voice when speaking with people in authority or in a position of power. I hear cries of, "I would never do that, what you see is what you get!" Think about the way you would speak to your mother; it is likely to be very different to the way you would speak to your best friends down at the pub or bar.

In order to build strong rapport with anyone you like, it is important to speak in a similar tone, pace, pitch, and timbre (quality) in which they speak. This is one of the most powerful techniques you can use to build strong rapport and is, of course, superb over the phone. You can even use these techniques in email because, as you will read in the next section, you can translate all the characteristics of your voice into the written word.

When you are talking to people, I want you to notice how they talk. Consider the following:

- Fast
- Slow
- Low pitch
- High pitch
- Monotone
- Melodious
- Emphasis on words or phrases
- Repetition of words or phrases
- Quality of their voice, e.g. rich, smooth, gravelly, squeaky
- Loud
- Quiet
- Rhythm
- Pace

Fall into step with them with your own voice. The easiest way is to follow the speed of their speech and drop in nuances they use, such as a hesitation, elongating words, or speaking quietly. Choose only a couple of things to follow and relax into it. Your voice will alter only slightly and your conversation will flow much more easily. You will know you are in rapport when the person you are talking to starts to say things like, "That resonates with me," or "I get you," or "I see what you mean," or they simply agree with you and say, "Yes."

Wherever you are and whatever you are doing, practice this very simple technique and it will get you further than you think because building rapport quickly and easily helps to build relationships quickly and easily and those lead to better opportunities for you.

Using this simple technique when you are emailing is effective, too. Here's how:

When you receive an email, notice how it starts, what the structure looks like, and how it ends. Some people love to send novels and some people will send one word. Both of these styles are an indication of how that person thinks; nothing more and nothing less. I have worked in some organizations where people get upset when they receive a short email in response to a very long email. This is because, for some reason, they think the person sending the short email is being rude. This is not true. For the most part, the person sending the short email is simply busy or is not a fan of long emails.

You need to alter your email style according to the style you have received. If the person wrote, "Hi," you write "Hi." If they start with "Dear," you start with "Dear," etc. It is the same with the sign-off. If they finish with "Best Regards," so do you.

Most people do not have time to read huge emails, so please do not send them. If you need to convey something complex, then pick up the phone and talk to the person or even better, go and see them. If the thing you need to convey needs to be in written form, then send it as a separate document to the email so that the person can open it and read it at their leisure.

Never send anything remotely emotional via email because it always ends badly. *Never* send an email in anger. Always walk away from the computer, take a break, go for a walk, or even sleep on it. The workplace is not the right place to vent your spleen by email. Emotional stuff needs to be covered face to face or over the phone. You have been warned!

Finally, remember that people will read and focus their attention on the first sentence and the last sentence of your email. They are less likely to take the middle bit on board so, where possible, keep it to bullet points (a maximum of five) to convey your message.

People will also read the "P.S." so, if you have got a key message that you want people to notice, put it in a postscript.

CHAPTER FIVE

Thinking for a Change

Whenever I coach chief executive officers (CEOs), who are the directors of senior managers, I am always amazed at how little time they devote to thinking. They seem to spend a great deal of time doing and taking on more and more tasks, but very little time in thinking about whether those tasks are necessary.

I encourage all of my coachees to find time in their busy lives to think. It does not matter whether this is on the journey to and from work, whether it is over a coffee halfway through the morning, or whether it is when you take the dog for a walk, the point is you allocate time to create space in your head.

Many of the best leaders I meet spend the time during their daily commute thinking about their people and their long-term strategy. It is one of the few places where they can find the peace and quiet to think properly.

I have already shown that using some simple techniques can help you to relax on purpose and I propose you use those techniques during your thinking time to allow thoughts to emerge. I often have thoughts pop into my head while I am cooking dinner or while I am travelling for work. When this happens, I write them down and leave them to develop like a good wine. Someone once told me that Sir Richard Branson sits in his hammock on his private island and thinks. When he gets an idea, he writes down all the stuff that can go wrong and weighs it up against all the stuff that can go right. If the right column massively outweighs the wrong column then he goes ahead and does it.

After reading this, I realized this is what I do, except it is usually on a rainy, windy day up Blackford Hill rather than in the Caribbean in a hammock!

Allocate time to thinking. At first, your colleagues and peers will think you are crazy, but they will disagree when they see your ideas adopted and your career or business take off. You do not need much time to think, either; half an hour here or there during a busy week is sufficient because it needs to balance with your action.

Sometimes, setting time aside to thinking is not enough, but neither is switching off your brain. There needs to be a different perspective in order to solve a problem, move forward, or create an opportunity. This is when some disassociation and association is required.

Association and disassociation are two NLP terms, but you do not need to worry about the long words because it is easy to get a new perspective when you know how.

Sit comfortably, somewhere safe and secure when you have five minutes to yourself. If you are very busy, then sit in your car before you drive or sit on the toilet – generally, no one will disturb you in either of these places (except if you are a parent of young children, in which case, the only place you will find peace and quiet is when they are fast asleep).

Make sure that you plant both feet firmly on the ground, sit up straight, take three deep breaths in through your mouth, and let them out through your nose. Relax. Once you have read these instructions, close your eyes, and begin to visualize yourself floating upwards.

Choose a method of floating upwards that makes you feel safe and secure because you are going up high. Float all the way up until you reach the edge of space and now look down onto yourself sitting where you are. When you look down on yourself, consider any issues or problems you have and, from this edge-of-space view, look around you and notice what resources you already have that can help you solve these issues. It is amazing how many people already have the resources they need to solve their problems and that looking at things from a different perspective really helps.

Now stay high and float off into your future with the knowledge that all the resources you need are in your past. Everything you ever learned, did, experienced, said, heard, or acknowledged is in your past. As you continue to float high and go off into your future in a safe and secure way, look down along your future time line and pick up all those new resources you need in order to attain your solution. Then float just beyond the time where you have your solution or imagine you have your solution and stop. Look down through your own eyes on yourself with your solution. Bounce down very briefly into your solution into the bounciest trampoline you have ever experienced and bounce straight back up again, bringing with you the resources you need. The answer to your solution is now with you, or if it is not, go out further into your future to the time when you have definitely nailed it. Bounce down again and bring your resources back with you.

Now equipped with the resources, float backwards along your time line, making note of all the steps you have taken to get to the solution, and bring all the resources with you to the present. Float gently back down into your chair knowing that you now have all the resources you need to solve your problem and achieve your goals.

It takes time to do, but only about five minutes, and it is well worth spending that time productively solving your issues.

There are more ways to alter your own perspective and, crucially, the perspective of others. This takes the form of questions to ask, but that is for a later chapter.

CHAPTER SIX

Having Presence

It is always nice to have presence, do you not think? My favorite is the birthday variety, but presents any time of year are good.

Seriously, having presence is one of those seemingly mysterious qualities that some people have and some people do not know how to get. It has nothing to do with size, shape, power, money, gender, or culture and has absolutely everything to do with an inner core of self-belief. I know very quiet CEOs who have enormous presence and when you speak to them, you know they have real wisdom that is worth listening to. I know a very tiny woman in business who commands a room of senior business leaders with one word and, conversely, I know of people who think they have presence because they wear a sharp suit and are in a position of power, yet no one takes any notice of them.

It is not about how loud or forceful you are; in fact, it is the opposite. I was chatting to a very senior business leader the other week at a networking event and someone who does similar work to me interrupted us. This person talked over me, aggressively contradicted me, and took over the conversation by shutting me out in order to make an impact on this senior business leader.

I stood back and allowed this person to dig her own hole, which she did very successfully. Instead of giving the impression of having presence, this individual gave the impression of desperation and the senior business leader switched off. I made my excuses, struck up a conversation with another group of people, and contemplated offering this person some help with their networking skills. I decided against it because this individual was not remotely aware that they were overbearing and rude and would not have taken kindly to my offer of help.

So, how do you go about creating presence for yourself without being overly forceful or seeming arrogant? As with everything in life, it is easy when you know how. Here are a few simple techniques that you can practice.

My teachers, John and Kathleen La Valle and Dr Richard Bandler, run a fantastic course in Florida called Charisma Enhancement. When you have finished reading this book, I recommend the course for those of you who wish to have more presence.

In the meantime, I will talk you through the way they taught me. Start by standing or sitting correctly: sitting up straight or standing with your feet hip-width apart and one foot at a slight 45-degree angle to the other. This gives you a firm platform and the ability to turn to every part of the room. It also has the effect of giving you a 3D image to the room rather than facing people straight on, which gives you a very flat profile. We have talked about eye contact and this is very much a part of having good presence. Make sure you look everyone in your audience in the eye at some point during the conversation. This applies to interviews, meetings, presentations, and talks.

As you stand or sit there and survey the scene, have these words running through your head: "Your ass is mine!" spoken in a Jack Nicolson-like cheeky grin with an air of steely determination behind it. Give yourself some devil horns to complete the image! Clearly, you need to practice this in your own head silently, unless you are alone in which case make it as dramatic and outlandish as you possibly can. You can view some of my YouTube videos on this subject by going to the Rebecca Bonnington YouTube Channel.

Breathe in and out, so that you are nice and relaxed, and then speak. If it is a big presentation, meeting, or interview, then use the nerves you might have to your advantage and remember that excitement and anticipation create those same feelings. It is an opportunity for learning and having fun. It is good to smile whenever you are speaking, as long as it is appropriate, and it is always good to introduce humor so that your message is absorbed. People learn and absorb much more when humor is used. However, use your best judgment to decide whether humor is appropriate in your context.

Allow others to speak and then say your piece. Keep your sentences nice and concise and do not ramble on. Always listen openly and actively using peripheral vision while you engage with others because this will help you keep your own mind clear, enable you to relax, and really listen to others well. Listening properly is a skill that all people with great presence have, but is sadly lacking in most organizations. When people feel you listen to them, they warm to you, respect you more, and tend to listen to you in return (although, not always).

As before, use a few key words and phrases spoken by the others in your conversation to demonstrate you are listening and that you are building rapport. It is usually good to clarify other people's points, too, using phrases such as:

"So, if I understand you correctly..."

"Would I be right in thinking that...?"

"If I have got this right, what you are saying is..."

Use your hands deliberately. This is something that brilliant orators do and is something you can replicate easily in everyday conversations at work and in business. Some people flail about with their hands while speaking and that is all very well and good if that is the way the people you are impressing use their hands. As with all kinds of rapport building, it is vital to minimise the differences between yourself and the person or key people with whom you are talking.

Here are some simple ideas to get you started:

1. When asking someone to listen, point to your ears.
2. When asking someone to consider various points, literally count the points on your fingers as you describe them.
3. When illustrating something, draw a frame in the air in front of you so that people you are speaking to will paint their own picture in the frame.
4. When you are saying, "I think," point to your head.
5. If you are presenting and you are asking people for questions, open your arms up and hold the palms of your hands out to the audience, as this is an inviting gesture.

Think of five more ways you can use your body language, especially your hands, when speaking to clearly define your point.

Why is this helpful? When you consider that many people think, learn, and observe in a visual way, your hand movements will help them understand what you say at a deeper level. Then consider that many people like to experience, walk through, touch, and feel before they completely understand or learn something, then your hand movements help them, too. Those who like to listen will hear you anyway and those who like to sit back, observe, and cogitate will be doing that, as well; you will just help everyone become engrossed in what you say.

When not using your hands to illustrate your chat, keep them happy and occupied with a light clasp together at the front or down by your side.

Know your stuff

It is absolutely true that empty vessels make the most noise. If you want respect in your field of expertise or area of business, then you must make it your life's work to become an expert in that arena. There are no short cuts to this, no magic tricks, and no wands to wave. This part takes hours of learning, listening, observing, studying, and modelling the existing experts in your chosen profession.

There are two things to consider here:

First, to have presence and command respect for your business acumen or your professional expertise, you must love passionately the thing that you do. When you love the thing that you do passionately, you never have to work another day in your life (personal conversation with John La Valle, 2012). Thus, the work you put in might be hard, but it enhances your passion ultimately, so it is worth it.

Second, if you are not passionate about what you do, go find something you are passionate about doing. If you are worried about paying the mortgage or supporting your family by pursuing your passion, then find a way to do it anyway. There is always a way if your passion is strong enough, even if it means making huge sacrifices to achieve it.

After I closed my recruitment business and gave up a generous salary, I had a choice: get a proper job with a salary, pension, and paid holidays or pursue the thing I was passionate about, i.e. learning and helping others to learn in business. I considered teaching to help me fulfil this passion, earn a salary, and get a pension. However, I knew that the other thing I was passionate about was freedom and the only way I could achieve that was to remain self-employed.

My lifestyle is great now. In the early days, though, I struggled to pay the most basic bills. To pursue your passion, you must first decide what is most important to you in life. Those people who have the greatest presence in the world of work and business have made huge personal sacrifices to achieve what they have. It is not an easy route, but it is liberating, fulfilling, life enhancing, and enriching.

Finally, whatever passion you are pursuing, remember you will make many mistakes. These "failures" are not really failures at all, but directions for change and learning. Picking yourself up, brushing yourself off, and starting again is the only answer to any setback you face. When you are passionate about what you do, picking yourself up and starting again is a no-brainer! People with presence admit when they are wrong; it takes great strength of character to do this. Any fool can cover up a mistake, but it takes depth of character to admit when you were wrong.

Real presence and passion go hand-in-hand; anything else is shallow and short-lived.

CHAPTER SEVEN

Asking the Right Questions to Get the Right Answers

Why, why, why-oh-why do people only have one way of asking a question? From a small age, "Why?" was probably your favorite question and it probably only got you so far in learning what you wanted to know before the information stopped coming after a certain number of repetitions. This is the same in the grown-up world of commerce. To wonder why is fantastic, to ask why is brilliant, and to have a whole range of questions to ask in lots of different ways to get better outcomes and information is transformational.

Let us have a real dig into the world of questions because asking the right questions in the right way opens up all kinds of wonderful doors of opportunity that in turn lead to success.

Why?

Use this when you want background information, a potted history if you like. For example:

"Why did you overlook me for promotion?"

"Why did you choose that top?"

"Why were you going there?"

When you ask, "Why?" you get lots of content and you often get well-rehearsed answers. People expect you to ask, so their answers are usually prepared in advance. This is not thinking in a quality way, this is reciting prepared material and, if that is what you are seeking, that is great. Sometimes that kind of data is really useful and interesting.

However, there is a range of questions that will help you to shift people's thinking from detail to big picture to abstract and back again at will. Imagine how useful it will be to get the person in IT or accounts who is obsessed with detail and cannot see the big picture to finally be able to grasp it? Alternatively, helping the creative people who love creating the vision but who often forget about the detail of delivering that vision.

I use these questions when helping to shift my clients' thinking. Sometimes I see their heads swivel round, literally, as they process the question in a different part of their brain. So often the light bulb flicks on and I can tell that their thinking has shifted. Some people laugh, some cry, and some drift off elsewhere while they process the questions and finally begin to think differently about their goals, ambitions, problems, and issues. Observing this massive shift in cognition is one of the best parts of my job!

Here's a little diagram to illustrate what I mean:

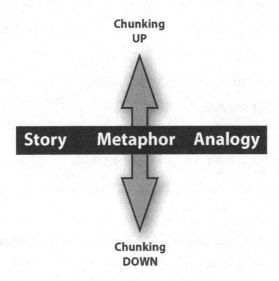

When you chunk up, you are enabling yourself and others to think about things from above, on a big scale, and in the macro. When you chunk down you are enabling yourself and others to think in detail, on a small scale, and in the micro.

Metaphor is a beautiful, gentle way to help people move effortlessly between the two. Metaphor helps enormously if someone does not quite understand the question or is stuck thinking in the big picture or in the detail. Remember, if you or anyone else has thought in a certain way for a long time, then you need a bit of help to readjust. Rest assured, though, that everyone can move about on this scale.

Once you have mastered this, you will be able to think on all levels effortlessly. You will be able to understand others' perspective quickly and easily and help them to understand an alternative view. Think about the transformation of meetings, interviews, sales calls, presentations, and performance reviews using this kind of skill.

Here are the questions the help people see the big picture, grasp the nettle, and hear the music:

1. For what purpose… *do you want this? …did you do this?*
2. How would it be if… *you learned a new skill? …we met for coffee to discuss this?*
3. What would happen if… *you succeed at the next interview? …they worked together as a team?*
4. What leads you to… *that conclusion? …believe that?*
5. How do you know… *that they would do that? …the company will grow?*
6. If you were to know…?

These are big questions and some people will answer them with detail. Persevere and ask follow on questions such as, "What else?" and "What will that give you?"

In big picture thinking, you are listening out for big, abstract concepts and ideas such as a vision, a big value, a thought, or something that might sound like *fulfilment, success,* or *growth*. These last three are often spoken about as though you could pick them up and put them in a wheelbarrow, which of course you cannot. However, we nominalize them and use these words as though they were nouns. This type of big, abstract description is what you want to hear when you are chunking up yourself or others.

When you want to chunk someone down, these are the questions you need to ask:

1. What specifically?
2. How exactly?
3. Describe in detail.
4. Who precisely?
5. Where exactly?

These are great questions when people say things such as, "Everyone does this," "This is how we have always done it here," or "No one knows how to do this," etc.

You might want to add a few more:

1. According to whom?
2. Who are "we"?
3. Where is it written that...?
4. How do you know?

Then, there are some vague enquiries to ask if you need help moving people around in their thinking or if you need to diffuse a situation:

1. I wonder if...
2. Can you help me...?
3. I am curious to know...

If you want to make it really vague to get a totally different response, here are some more:

1. I wonder whether you were to know how that would work.
2. Can you help me understand how to find a way to work that?

These last two sound very vague and a bit confusing. This is a good thing, particularly when you want to take someone out of their thinking groove; confusing someone is a great way to do that because they have to stop, reverse, and recalculate their position.

Use these questions on yourself first to find out what difference they make to your regular thinking patterns. Have a go at some simple questions, then change them around using these techniques, and observe what happens.

1. Where do you live?
2. For what purpose do you live there?
3. What leads you to believe this is a good place for you to live?
4. How did you know to live there?

5. What specifically drew you to live there?

6. Where exactly do you live?

7. Can you help me understand where you live?

8. I am wondering where you live.

9. Why do you live there?

10. How would it be if you lived somewhere else?

11. What would happen if you did not live there?

12. If you were to know, where else would you live?

You will notice how each question moves your thinking in different directions and although you are answering pretty much the same question, you have to think in slightly different ways to answer each question.

How useful is that in interviewing, meetings, appraisals, coaching, and presentations? Very.

The Wonderful World of And, So, As, While, and Because

When you hear people speak or when you read their words, often the little words have the biggest impact because as you read or listen you will notice that there is a rhythm to the way people write or speak. Learning the skills of identifying patterns of speech and language will be a great tool in your armory.

Read this sentence again:

When you hear people speak or when you read their words, often the little words have the biggest impact. When you read or listen, you sometimes notice that there is a rhythm to the way people write or speak. However, learning those skills of identifying patterns of speech and language can be a great tool in your armory.

What do you notice? Read both paragraphs aloud and listen to the difference between the two.

The first one is more soporific (it sends you to sleep) and the second one is more jilted and keeps you awake. The second one also creates doubt in your mind that people have rhythm in their language and seems to suggest that learning these skills might be difficult. Conversely, the first paragraph presupposes that you will learn these tools and it flows with much more ease.

When you speak or write, using words such as *and, so, because, while* or *as* help you to build a gentle rhythm so that the listener or reader is lulled by your words. You might be wondering why you would want people to be lulled by your words; sometimes you do not. The best orators of our age speak in rhythms and they capture a flow, which people will listen to gladly for hours. After hearing Bill Clinton speak when he came to Glasgow, I can tell you honestly that I have no idea what he said exactly, but I thought he was great and he certainly captured the imagination of the five hundred business people in the room.

Simon Sinek, in his TEDTalk, "How great leaders inspire action," speaks about the fact that people make decisions based on their emotions (Sinek, 2009). When you talk to a group of people or an individual, you want them to warm to you emotionally because then they are more likely to like you, promote you, listen, or buy from you. Speaking in a flowing, gentle rhythm that enables people to relax when they are listening to you is a great skill to possess.

Sometimes, of course, you really do want to speak or write in a staccato, boom-boom fashion. These are in times of crisis, emergency, or when you need to grab people's attention quickly. Like a command-and-control style in leadership, though, use this sparingly, as no one likes listening to a machine gun and people switch off at the third command you have given them.

But and However

"Today's meeting was fantastic; we all got a lot out of it, but next time we need to..."

"Your progress, to date, has been amazing. However, you could try doing..."

Grrr! So many people in business give fantastic praise and then immediately negate it by saying *but* or *however*. These two little words wipe out the lovely praise completely, to the extent that you may as well not have said it.

Here is how to deliver praise and constructive criticism at the same time:

"Today's meeting was fantastic because we all got a lot out of it so, next time, let us..."

"Your progress, to date, has been amazing and I would love you to..."

What a difference with replacing the *but* and *however* with *because* and *and*. You can also use *while* and *as* for the same effect.

Practice these questions and the use of *and, as, while,* and *because* and notice what happens to your communication and the responses you get. It is wonderful.

Figure legend

Figure 7.1 Big picture, little picture.

CHAPTER EIGHT

Being Bendy

Remember the picture of the tree at the beginning of the book? Here is a reminder.

I have given you this model again because it is the one I draw when I talk about building in behavioral flexibility and altering your behavior depending on who you are talking to and what situation you are in. People often ask whether that is an authentic way of being or whether you are just out to manipulate people by pretending to be someone you are not.

One of the reasons I got you to consider your core values right at the beginning is because those represent you as a human being. They are your core, your non-negotiable "this is me" and "this is who I am" values. They root you to your reality, inform your choices, and enable you to find contentment when those values match those of your partner and your work. That is the secret to a successful and happy life: matching your core values to the values of the people with whom you spend your time and what you do every day is the not-so-secret secret of happiness.

Sticking to these core values enables you to have flexibility in your behavior because behavior is simply a reflection of what is going on in your world and your head at any one point. Here is an example:

I love people. I spend my working life talking to people, helping people, and writing about them. The love of helping others learn is a core value of my business. When I go on holiday, though, I only spend time with my family. I have absolutely no interest whatsoever in making friends, socializing outside my family, or even talking to other people beyond the social niceties. If you only ever met me when I was on holiday, you would think I was polite, but quiet and slightly aloof. My friends at home and anyone I meet in business would describe me as exactly the opposite and, yet, it is still me. My values are precisely the same, but my behavior – what the outside world observes – is very different at work compared to when I am on holiday with my family.

This is because for two weeks every summer and one week at New Year, I completely and utterly switch off from people, which gives me the energy I need to return to work full of enthusiasm.

I talked briefly about modifying your behavior in the doctor's consulting room and changing your language in other formal situations. As you climb the career ladder or develop your business, you will need to be flexible in your behavior. Great leaders have a repertoire ranging from command-and-control in a crisis (think of an army major) to relaxed democrat when things are going well.

This comes across in your language, voice, and body language. You are all different and I encourage you to utilize your range of behavior as you encounter different situations and different people around you.

Remember Fred Goodwin from The Royal Bank of Scotland (RBS)? He was a great example of someone who had only one way of behaving: he was a dictatorial micro-manager. He got involved in the tiniest of details during the building of the massive RBS headquarters in Edinburgh, right down to the type of trees planted in the centre of the building known as The Street. His leadership style consisted of telling people what to do and, so, when he left, no one knew what they were supposed to do because no one had had to think for themselves for such a long time. He was toppled because of his inflexibility. He refused to listen to anyone's advice because he stuck to one way of being.

I have no idea whether he learned his lesson. Dictators often do not. Think about the flexibility of the behavior of someone like Gandhi: steadfast to his values and prepared to be flexible in his behavior to achieve those values. Great leaders have this fantastic combination of being able to stick to a path, provide direction, boundaries, and vision, while behaving in a way that allows them to chat happily to the receptionist about their weekend one minute and reprimand a failing director the next.

Many of the techniques I have described in this book will help you build that behavioral range and by attending a good quality NLP practitioner course such as my own or any other run by someone qualified by The Society of Neuro-Linguistic Programming will enable you to achieve that at a completely new level.

Figure legend

Figure 8.1 Understanding your values and more.

CHAPTER NINE

Taking Control

There are two types of attitude among people in this world: *cause* and *effect*.

Here is the lowdown on the two. When you are in *cause*, you are like this:

- Empowered
- 100% responsible for *everything* that happens in your life
- In control of yourself
- A master of your mood, emotions, and thought
- Free

When you are in *effect*, you are like this:

- Disempowered
- Unable to accept responsibility or blame
- A victim of your emotions, moods and thinking
- Out of control of yourself
- Incarcerated

Cause is a great place to be and it is where all successful people live. The other is a horrible place to be and it is where people live who spend their lives wishing things could be different.

Nelson Mandela was imprisoned for decades, often in the harshest and most inhumane conditions, and yet he remained free in his head. He controlled his thinking and he decided what attitude and what emotions he would maintain. Sometimes he lost it and had to work hard to get back on track. Ultimately, though, he forgave his incarcerators and he forgave the system that put him there. Despite being imprisoned physically, he remained free mentally because he took 100% responsibility for himself and his state of mind.

So many people are free and yet they place cages of steel around themselves: "It is too hard," "I cannot do it," "People like me do not do stuff like that," "I do not have the money," "I am too old/fat/tall/short/dark/pale/pink/blue," etc.

When you consider that reasons and excuses are exactly the same thing, you begin to realize that the only thing stopping you from doing what you want to do is yourself.

Let us take the money and time issue first because these are classic ones. I have three children, a husband, a dog, and I run my own business. Time is precious to me. Yet, I completed a master's degree and now I am writing a book. I still earn decent money and I am able to provide for my children.

When people tell me that they do not have time, I ask them what they do each evening. It turns out that there is usually at least one hour each evening that they could set aside to pursuing their passion. They usually have at least one afternoon or a couple of hours at the weekend, too. Instead of wasting time watching TV, surfing the net, or posting to Facebook, you could be using that time to pursue your passion, practice your skills, and develop new talents or skills.

Money: if people who are impoverished can save the meager resources they have, then so can you. What do you spend on clothes, shoes, handbags, going out, drinks, the gym, coffees, cigarettes, presents, cards, food, petrol, cars, satellite TV, gadgets?

There are *always* sacrifices you can make to save some money to help you achieve what you want. Go and borrow a self-help guide to saving money book from the library – it is free!

Even if you can only save £10 per week, you will have £520 at the end of the year to put towards the pursuit of your passion. If you cannot save £10 per week, then save £5 or £1 and sell all the things you do not use.

"But," I hear you cry, "I have a really busy, demanding job and do not feel like tackling my novel in the evenings, or I know I should read up on professional selling skills, but..." etc. These are all excuses, full stop. You either want to be the best in your career and business or you do not.

Someone told me a story the other week about two nurses. They happened to be related. One nurse was off to visit The Royal Household and receive her MBE from Prince Charles at Buckingham Palace, while the other nurse grumped and moaned about how unfair it was that her relative got all the glory from doing the same job.

It is true that they did the same job and to the same level of expertise. This is where the similarity stops, though, because the nurse getting the MBE also spent her free time learning, researching, and writing ground-breaking papers and books on her area of expertise and on how to bring about massive improvements for patients. Apparently, this nurse's work is now used throughout the NHS and is considered best practice.

One nurse sacrificed her spare time and her holidays to help modernize her profession and the other grumped and moaned about it.

When you have finally got fed up of hearing your own voice moan about your boss, your work, your organization, or your relationship, then you might just decide to do something about it because here is the thing: *no one else* is going to do anything about it.

When you are whining and whinging, you are in effect. The moment you take the decision to do something about it and then *do it*, you are in cause and you are on the road to total personal freedom.

It took me three years to find the courage to leave an abusive relationship. The man I was with was an alcoholic and I realized that my own mental state was being affected negatively by staying with him.

I was often ill with mysterious viruses and eventually I got skin cancer: a malignant melanoma, the most virulent kind. My dermatologist could not work out why I had developed it because I never used sun beds and did not live or travel abroad as a child. She agreed with me that stress was probably the cause. Thus, ten years of being in an unhappy relationship, with the final three years being almost unbearable, took their toll on my frame of mind and my physical well-being.

Leaving was the hardest thing I had ever done and raising two young children on my own while running a business was the second hardest. Yet, they were liberating in the extreme because I was finally in control.

Remember that when you are in cause, you must take 100% responsibility for everything that happens in your life. If the banks collapse the day after you set up your new business, you need to take responsibility for succeeding in really tough times or put it on hold and work somewhere else. If you are made redundant, fall ill, or find yourself in difficult times, it is your responsibility to get yourself out of it. Ask for help, accept help offered, learn from others, take time to recover, and maybe adjust your path because we do not always get precisely what we want. However, we can always take responsibility for how we deal with difficulties.

When the deals or the projects go wrong, stand-up, take responsibility for your part in them. Getting ahead in the world of business is about admitting when you made a mistake and working out how to succeed next time.

My recruitment business failed and I took full responsibility for that. My first marriage failed and I took responsibility for my part in that, too. My record with boyfriends was not the best and I took responsibility for that. The common denominator in my life is me! I am the only constant, so when it is good or bad it is down to me and the part I play.

Some people say that you cannot take responsibility for finding yourself in a plane crash, run over by a drunk driver, raped, or attacked. Those people would be quite right; you cannot control the actions of other people.

However, after the event, you can absolutely take responsibility for how you deal with it. As with all things I wonder and think about, I started writing this section yesterday and last night watched a TEDTalk by Janine Shepherd (Shepherd, 2012). I urge you to watch it as her story illustrates my point beautifully. For those of you who might not get around to watching it, here is a synopsis:

Janine was training for the Olympics. She was extremely fit and being an athlete was her life. She was cycling the last ten minutes of a five-hour bike ride through the Blue Mountains in Australia and she was enjoying her uphill cycle into the glorious mountain ahead. Then her world went black and she found herself in an intensive care ward, unable to move. A speeding truck had driven into her.

She had multiple injuries, half her face was missing, four ribs and an arm were broken, her spine was crushed, and she had massive internal bleeding. She lost nearly all her blood and she was at death's door. For ten days, Janine describes how she struggled to stay alive as her body wanted to give up, but her mind (unconscious/spirit) did not and she made the decision to come back, at which point her internal bleeding stopped.

She recovered enough to make it home six months later. She was confined to a wheel chair and was paralyzed from the waist down. She was still wearing a body cast and a catheter. This was not the life she anticipated. Her body no longer worked and her body had defined her. It had been her whole identity. She fell into a depression.

One day though, she describes how she watched a plane fly over her house and how she decided in that moment that she could not walk, but she could fly. She grabbed the phone book and booked her first flying lesson.

It took her eighteen months of hard work, determination, sweat, and tears to get to the point in her life where not only is she now a pilot, but she is an acrobatic display pilot and, indeed, teaches other people to fly and do acrobatic displays. She walks unaided and no longer has a body cast or catheter.

Taking 100% responsibility for everything that happens in your life might be a scary prospect at first, but once you get used to the idea, it is hugely liberating because it means you can go ahead and achieve anything you like, so long as it is good for you and the people around you. Whether or not you achieve it is all up to you and that is an amazing feeling.

CHAPTER TEN

Making the Best Decisions

Hindsight is a wonderful thing that we sometimes wish we had before we took a decision! There is no point in beating yourself up over decisions you made in the past because you made the best decision you could at the time with the information and resources you had available at that point. Had you known then what you know now, it might have been different, but you did not, so stop your nonsense and move on!

There is a way, though, to test a decision before you make it. You can work out whether the decision you are about to make is a good one beforehand. Gut feeling is usually a good indicator, but many people are not in tune with that and do not yet trust it. Experience and knowledge helps, too, but can also be a red herring. How can you be sure that the decision you are about to take is going to be a good one? This is how:

Think about a decision you made in the recent past regarding a minor purchase you made. Make sure it is small, inexpensive, and does not carry much meaning to it. A coffee maker, a pair of boots, a jacket would be good examples. A house, car, or holiday would not.

Take a piece of paper and write down your answers to the following questions:

1. When you think about the item you purchased, is the image you make in color or in black and white?
2. Is this image moving or still?
3. What size is the image?
4. What distance is the image from you?
5. Is the image three-dimensional or flat?
6. Are you in the image or looking at it through your own eyes?
7. Are there any sounds associated with your purchase?
8. If there are, what are the volume, tone, pitch, and pace of the sounds?
9. Are the sounds in your left ear, right ear, or both?
10. If the sounds are voices, to whom do they belong?
11. What are the feelings associated with this purchase?
12. Where in your body do you experience those feelings?
13. What is the intensity of the feelings?
14. Are there any colors or shapes associated with the feelings?
15. Do the feelings spin? If so, which way do they spin?

Put that piece of paper to one side and get a clean sheet of paper.

Now think about another purchase you made, again inexpensive, mundane, and with little emotion attached. Choose something you thoroughly enjoy owning, something that gives you enormous pleasure every time you use it, look at it, or touch it. Answer the same fifteen questions listed above on your clean sheet of paper.

Now, place the two pieces of paper side by side and with a different colored pen or highlighter pen, identify the key differences in your answers.

It is these key differences in your decision making process that you need to be aware of in the future because these are the differences that will improve the quality of your decisions for the rest of your life.

Test this process out. Choose a more significant decision you have made in the past that did not go at all well and run it through the same fifteen questions. Then choose a great, life-enhancing decision and compare the two.

Again, you will notice that there are key differences. You now have a clear idea of what a bad decision looks, feels like, and sounds like to you, as well as what a good decision looks like, feels like, and sounds like. This is useful information that you need to learn, keep with you, and use whenever you are going to make a decision in life or work.

If you are at a crossroads in your life, or simply need to make a career or business decision, then run through these questions with your options. Consider the options available to you and "try them on" for a while. Live for a few days or a week as though you had made one of the decisions and experience how it sits with you.

Make sure you use the questions to pinpoint the key differences between the options. Then live with the alternative for a while and run through the questions with it.

This process will really help you understand how you make the best decisions for yourself. These decisions may not please everyone, but pleasing everyone is a fruitless task that only serves to drive you crazy. I once tried pleasing everyone when I was the managing director of my own business and, I can tell you, it ended in tears – mostly my tears – and no one was happy.

This is a very personal process and the responses will be very different for everyone so do not compare yourself with others. Go with your own good decision making strategy, learn how you make good decisions, and keep doing it. Use this process in your working and your personal life because it works well whatever you are deciding. What happens, eventually, is that you get to know very quickly whether the decision you are about to make is good, bad, or indifferent and you no longer need to go through the questions. It is at this point you will finally be listening to your gut instinct because your gut instinct knew all along what the right decision was, you just were not listening closely enough.

CHAPTER ELEVEN

Making It Happen

You have now set your objectives, you have put them in your timeline, you have cleared up anything that has been holding you back, you have changed your language and you have used your brain: this all very well and good. Now, you need to take massive action because the process you have just been through has made your brain ready for serious action. Your neurology is fired up, ready to get going, so your actions need to be congruent with your thinking.

There are plenty of dreamers out there who talk a good game. They might even go on retreats, courses, or follow paths of learning to get where they want to be, but they never quite get there because they miss the last piece of the jigsaw puzzle.

Signing up to study for a master's degree in coaching was only the first step towards obtaining my degree; actually doing the reading, writing the assignments, and completing my dissertation were the massive action steps I had to take to graduate.

Taking an NLP Trainer training course in Florida was amazing, but actually booking a venue, marketing my courses, and attracting attendees was the massive action I needed to take to achieve my dream of training people in NLP.

There are countless examples of dreamers who had great intentions and fantastic ideas but never actually achieved anything. While your action might be massive, as I have said before in this book, you can take baby steps. Taking a small step each day or taking time each day to devote to your objectives is all it takes because each of those tiny steps creates one big step, eventually.

As I edit this book, I notice that this is precisely the process I am going through right now to get it published. Each day, I do a little bit more work to get it closer to publication. I have managed to review about two chapters a day so far and it is amazing how quickly that adds up to a whole book.

Comparing yourself to yourself is the only comparison worth making as you progress through your steps. I have a client who compares himself to other CEOs and finds himself lacking. This is not surprising because other CEOs are different, have had different upbringings, think differently, behave differently, and have had different opportunities presented to them.

It really is pointless comparing yourself to anyone except you because each of us is unique. What is an amazing milestone for one person is an everyday occurrence for another. Think of Olympic athletes and their Paralympic counterparts. I work occasionally for a mental health charity and the things that some of my clients achieve are outstanding for them, but would be very ordinary for my corporate clients.

The way I gauge my own progress is to consider where I was a year ago and where I was a year ago is very different to where I am now, in terms of my professional career. There is no such thing as an overnight success in life and work. Even winners of *The X-Factor* have had to work hard to get a place in the show, never mind win it. With our media on 24 hours per day, it does appear that people achieve overnight success, but this is an illusion. They do not. What you never get to see is the long hours of learning their craft, making mistakes, and failing from time to time. We get to witness the gold medal winners, but we never see the years of blood, sweat, and tears that they go through to achieve that moment of glory.

This is why it is so important that what you are striving for is a deeply held passion. You will experience tough times on your path to success and so you will need to find strength in what you are doing in order to drive you. Giving up may cross your mind, but holding onto your passion will set you back on the right track. Pursuing the things you love doing, no matter what life throws at you, becomes a no-brainer because it is at the core of who you are. Taking action to achieve those goals also becomes a part of your daily existence because you simply cannot help but want to achieve your dreams.

When you look back at the notes you have taken while working your way through this book, you will surprise yourself at how much you have changed already. You will begin to realize that the only thing that has been holding you back is yourself. If reading this the first time around and working through the exercises has not got you quite where you want to be, go back, start again, or dip into the areas that need work and keep going. The right path for you may not be easy, but it is certainly worth the effort.

If you are going to live a full life, make sure you are living it with your ladder firmly against the correct wall. Ask yourself how much more pleasure and joy you can take in your life. How much more do you want to succeed and what else would you like to be enjoying right now?

CHAPTER TWELVE

Keeping It Fun

At several points in this book, I might have got a bit serious because sometimes that is appropriate; however, life is to be enjoyed. Life is there to experience pleasure, love, kindness, and sharing. We are here to help ourselves, and each other, lead fulfilled and wonderful lives – yes, even in the workplace. You are there to make your clients' lives easier or to help the production line run more smoothly or to simply help someone in a small way every day by keeping the street clean. It does not matter what you do, in some way you are there to help others (with the exception of criminality!).

Take pleasure and joy in what you do. Find the thing that keeps you there and focus on that. Find the fun, the laughter, and the joy in your work. This may come from colleagues, clients, or suppliers; it does not matter from where. Laugh as often as you are able, smile at people, and make them feel good for no reason at all. Even when you are out and about shopping, say thank you to people who serve you, be polite to those who provide you with goods and services, and always let someone know when they have done a good job. Not only will you feel good, but they will feel good, too. It takes mere moments to do this and, yet, so many people do not remember to do it. Spreading happiness is easy and it is free. It is an international commodity unavailable on any stock market and no one owns it except us.

Outshining the rest is about setting yourself apart from the average. You do not need to be Einstein to do this and neither do you need to be at the top of your game in terms of skill or qualification. What you need is to be a great person with whom to work, i.e. someone who is easily understood and who understands others, too. Being yourself is a great place to start and, with the added skills you learned in this book, you can be yourself while having fantastic flexibility in your behavioral styles, too.

Outshining the rest is not a popularity contest, either. It is about being true to your values and, thus, gaining the respect of those around you. You cannot be all things to all people as you grow your business or climb the career ladder, but you can be true to who you are and what you stand for, which makes you an attractive person with whom to work.

There is never an excuse for rudeness. Be polite.

Whenever you can, be kind, helpful, bring joy, and smile. It is your duty as a human being on this planet to do so. It also has the added benefit of making you feel really good about yourself and feeling really good about yourself is a great place to start making massive changes. So, go ahead and laugh – you will love it.

EPILOGUE

There is always more to learn about yourself and the world around you. It really does not matter how you go about learning as long as you are doing it in a positive and wholesome way that is good for both you and the people around you.

My journey is a continuous one. Each day there is something new I need to learn. Each client I work with teaches me something new and, each time I refresh my own NLP learning, I discover something new, too. Neuroscience has shown us that our brains are elastic, which means that we can continue learning right up until the day we die. When we are young, our little brains act likes sponges, absorbing as much as they possibly can from the world around us. As we get older, some people seem to switch off this curiosity and adopt unhelpful beliefs such as "You can't teach old dog new tricks." Well, science has proved that you can. Our brains are constantly firing off new sparks and creating new pathways when we come across something new and, so long as we continue to light up our thinking with new things, our brains will continue to stretch.

A long time ago, I decided that I did not have a comfort zone anymore. The world is too big a place to hide away inside myself. I decided that

I would be open to all kinds of new experiences because that way I could learn so much more. Beyond your comfort zone is where the magic really happens. It is where you make the biggest mistakes, it is where you fall flat on your face, but it is also where you push yourself beyond your perceived limits and experience true joy, true fulfilment, and true peace with yourself. Begin to love yourself and then you can share this with others. Share your knowledge freely, be kind every day, and open your eyes, hearts, and minds to the world around you because it is waiting for you.

RESOURCES

References

When referring to the work of Dr Richard Bandler, John La Valle, or Kathleen La Valle I am using the following sources:

NLP Seminars Group International Training Courses, www.purenlp.com

Specifically, the training manuals associated with the following courses:

NLP Practitioner, 2012

NLP Master Practitioner, 2008

NLP Licensed Trainer, 2012

Bandler, Richard. *Get the Life You Want: the Secrets to Quick & Lasting Life Change*. London: Harper Element, 2009.

Bandler, Richard. *Richard Bandler's Guide to Trance-formation: Make Your Life Great*. London: Harper Element, 2010.

Clark, Jonathan. NLP Training. http://jonathanclark.org/nlp-scotland.

Cuddy, A. (2012, June). Amy Cuddy: Your body language shapes who you are [Video file]. Retrieved from http://www.ted.com/talks/amy_cuddy_your_body_language_shapes_who_you_are.html

Einstein, Albert. BrainyQuote.com, Xplore Inc, 2014. http://www.brainyquote.com/quotes/quotes/a/alberteins148778.html, accessed January 29, 2014.

Shepherd, J. (2012, October). Janine Shepherd: A broken body isn't a broken person [Video file]. Retrieved from http://www.ted.com/talks/janine_shepherd_a_broken_body_isn_t_a_broken_person.html

Sinek, S. (2009, September) Simon Sinek: How great leaders inspire action. [Video file]. Retrieved from http://www.ted.com/talks/simon_sinek_how_great_leaders_inspire_action.html

Thomson, Garner with Khan, Khalid. *Magic in Practice: Introducing Medical NLP - The Art and Science of Language in Healing and Health*. London: Hammersmith Press Limited, 2008.

Wright, Heather. Advance Performance. http://www.advance-performance.co.uk.

Ziglar, Zig. BrainyQuote.com, Xplore Inc, 2014. http://www.brainyquote. com/quotes/quotes/z/zigziglar125675.html, accessed January 29, 2014.

Recommended reading and further learning

I heartily recommend any training delivered by Dr Richard Bandler and John and Kathleen La Valle. Visit www.purenlp.com for more details of their courses in the USA.

Visit www.nlplifetraining.com for UK courses.

If you want to learn NLP with me, you are very welcome and you can find a list of my courses by visiting www.rebeccainspires.com.

If you would like me to come into your organization and coach or train your people then you can contact me at rebecca@rebeccainspires. com. I am also happy to speak at conferences.

Further reading includes:

Bandler, Richard. *Richard Bandler's Guide to Trance-formation: Make Your Life Great.* London: Harper Element, 2010.

Bandler, Richard and La Valle, John. *Persuasion Engineering: Sales and Business, Sales and Behavior.* California: Meta Publications, 1996.